D1609263

Bc

HQ 759 .V34 1978
Vaughn, Ruth.
  To be a mother : a daughter's
definition of and tribute to a mother
who stood with her child in each

To Be A Mother

To Be A Mother

*A daughter's definition of and tribute
to a mother who stood with her child
in each season and in each time
under the heaven*

Ruth Vaughn

THOMAS NELSON INC., PUBLISHERS

NASHVILLE · NEW YORK

HQ
759
.V34
1978

Scripture quotations are from the King James Version of the Bible.

Copyright 1978 by Ruth Vaughn

All rights reserved under International and Pan-American Conventions. Published in Nashville, Tennessee, by Thomas Nelson Inc., Publishers and simultaneously in Don Mills, Ontario, by Thomas Nelson & Sons (Canada) Limited. Manufactured in the United States of America.

Book Design by Nancy Bozeman

Photographs by Jim Whitmer

Library of Congress Cataloging in Publication Data

Vaughn, Ruth.
  To be a mother.

  1. Mothers. 2. Parent and child. I Title.
HQ759.V34   301.42′7   78–17201
ISBN 0–8407–5144–3

In
Memory of My Mother

MRS. S. L. WOOD

Who dialogued with me through my life, not in these exact
words, but in essence.
This is the way I remember the impact of the lady who
stood with me in each season and in each
time under the heaven.

Contents

Prologue

10

He was dressed in white the first time I saw
him—white diaper, white gown. Only his blanket was
the traditional blue.

He looked up at me with solemn eyes.

I returned his gaze with equally serious
demeanor.

He was changing my life.

He was forcing me from the role
of young girl and
carefree bride
to
that awesomely responsible
role of
mother.

"What kind of mother are you going to be?" his
probing eyes demanded.

I swallowed hard.

I had no idea what kind of mother I would be.

True, I wanted to be a good one,
but could I?

Young, imperfect me?

I doubted it.

My somber eyes stared back
into his.

I could not answer his question.

When they took him away, I was troubled.

I stood on the threshold of a world for which I was ill-equipped, ill-prepared, ill-rehearsed.

I was only twenty, just out of college—yet I was a mother. And my son had lain in my arms, searching my face for an answer to his future. What kind of mother would I be?

In the days that followed, I searched for an answer.

My only point of reference was my own mother.

But my heart sank with despair when I thought of her.

She was gentle, loving, and long-suffering.

I knew I could never be like that!

She was a perfect mother—but sad as it may be, perfect mothers breed imperfect daughters. I knew with certainty I could not be a perfect mother to my son.

What then?

Concede that motherhood was a job I could not handle and send him back?

No! Even if that were possible, I knew I would not do that. I had already seen him, held him, and felt his love reaching to me. I wanted to be his mother more than anything in the world. So . . . if I were going to keep him, what kind of mother would I be?

My heart wanted to cry out, "A good mother, a perfect mother!"

But honesty held me back.

Much as I wanted to, I knew I could not be that kind of mother to my son.

I could electrify an audience with my portrayal of Rebecca; I could stroll across the stage, dramatically reciting "Patterns" by Amy Lowell; I could write a prize-winning essay. But those things were irrelevant now. I faced the immortal challenge of motherhood, and I found myself inadequate for the task.

And so the tears came in great convulsive sobs.

After a few moments, my husband bounced into the room with all the exuberance of new fatherhood. Upon seeing my tears, he stopped abruptly. "Is something wrong with the baby?"

13

I shook my head woefully.

"No, there is something wrong with the mother."

He listened quietly to my confession that although I wanted to be a perfect mother to his son, I could not be.

When I finished, he grinned.

GRINNED!

"Men never understand," I thought.

And then he said something wise.

"You probably won't be 'perfect' like your mother. Remember you are only twenty; this is your first child. Your mother was forty-three when you were born; you were the eighth child. Mothers surely improve with age and experience.

"Be fair. Accept yourself for what you are. All I—and our son—ask is that you be the best mother *you* can be."

He kissed me then, teased me about my red nose (always luminous when I cry), and went away.

I felt better.

Perhaps this was the key: Accept myself as I was. Strive to be the best mother I could be at age twenty with my first child. Imperfect I would be—but I would try—and surely mothers *do* improve with age and experience! Therein lay my hope.

I grabbed a piece of paper and began to scribble:

Resolved: to be the best mother I can be.

I chewed thoughtfully on the eraser. Perhaps I should define my terms more explicitly. Maybe I should try to spell out my answer to the question: "What is a mother?"

This book contains the answer that I have chosen for myself through the years. Failing often, weak always, imperfect as I am, this is the goal of motherhood for which I strive.

A Mother Is God's Greatest Creation

A mother is God's assistant during the delicate process of building character in those eternal personalities entrusted to her.

She spends her life mothering neighbors, cats, and children; patching jeans, curtains, and broken hearts; cooking cornbread, oatmeal, and hot dogs; supervising the ironing, floor waxing, and shoe shining; teaching goodness, obedience, and the multiplication table.

She fills each moment with creating small dresses from large ones, stew from nothing, and curtains from worn sheets; training voices, animals, and babies; directing piano practice, lesson study, and Junior's ABC's; counting sheets, children, and calories; rolling cupcakes in coconut, dough into piecrust, and stringy hair into golden curls.

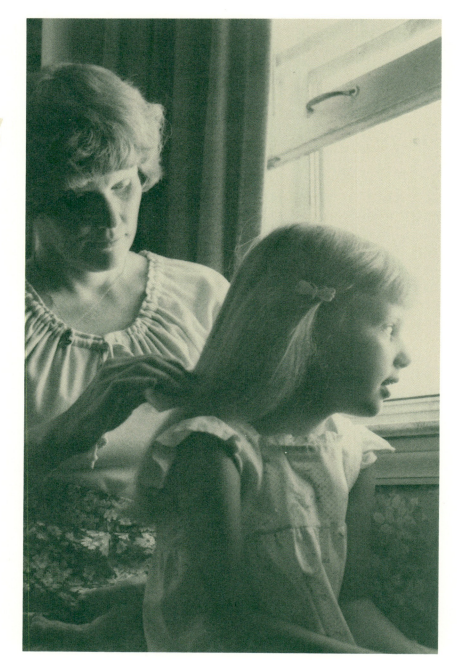

16

What Is A Mother?

A mother is always available for pushing red wagons, rope swings, and lifting everyone's spirits; moderating in times of anger, strife, and scratching; illustrating Bible stories, understanding, and the love of God; running to clean the kitchen, rescue the baby, and play "Red Rover"; making chocolate pies, tucks, ruffles, and peace, mending socks, songbooks, and shattered dreams; molding clay, gelatin, and young lives; feeding prim little girls, mischievous little boys, and innumerable puppies.

A mother is always capable of smiling despite illness, lack of sleep, and worn dresses; whispering prayers, encouragement, and love; smoothing difficult situations, ruffled feelings, and fevered brows; answering the telephone, the doorbell, and arithmetic problems; hiding her own disappointments, her longings, and Christmas presents; weeping in sorrow, in joy, and over a sick kitten; delivering food to the needy, children to school, and Father to work; loving animals, books, and all humanity; snatching moments to write poetry, paint pictures, and memorize Scripture.

A mother is never too busy to bake one more cake, plan a party, or listen to a glowing account of the teen-ager's last date; she is never too tired to sing a duet, count time for a recital piece, or advise someone in need of help.

She is never too rushed to smile as she mops the

floor, bakes cookies for Cub Scouts, or fixes a midnight snack; she is never too exasperated to tease about forgotten costumes for a rehearsal, grin when plans fall through, or make a joke of the situation when company comes and the cupboard is bare.

A mother can be found doing everything: changing diapers, reading stories, baking cakes, dissolving aspirin, camouflaging onions, gingerly accepting the gift of a wriggly worm, playing ball, attending the P.T.A., picking up toys, teaching a course on "How to Tell Time," singing lullabies, and spanking naughty children.

A mother likes bright sheets, sparkling dishes, and clean ears. She never spares tenderness, understanding, or the rod; she never fails to wipe runny noses, rub cold feet, or kiss good night. A mother can always be counted on for laughter, gentleness, discipline, firmness, and love.

A mother loves beauty, God, and children. She teaches by precept and example the wonder of salvation, the responsibilities of life, and the true meaning of love. She is "instant in season, out of season," reproving rebuking, exhorting with all long-suffering.*

A mother is adaptable. A different role, temper, and strength are required of her in each season and in each time under heaven.**

*2 Timothy 4:2
**Ecclesiastes 3:1

20 *A Time for Everything*

To everything there is a season, and a time to every purpose under the heaven:

A time to be born, and a time to die; a time to plant, and a time to pluck up that which is planted;

A time to kill, and a time to heal; a time to break down, and a time to build up;

A time to weep, and a time to laugh; a time to mourn, and a time to dance;

A time to cast away stones, and a time to gather stones together; a time to embrace, and a time to refrain from embracing.

A time to get away, and a time to lose; a time to keep and a time to cast away;

A time to rend, and a time to sew; a time to keep silence, and a time to speak;

A time to love, and a time to hate; a time of war, and a time of peace. . . .

He hath made everything beautiful in his time.

—Ecclesiastes 3:1–8, 11

21

22   *A Time to Be Born*

When I was sixteen, my mother gave me this letter. I had just come in from my birthday party and had collpased on the bed in a heap of ruffled skirt and brown curls. She grinned ruefully at my disarray as she handed me the letter.

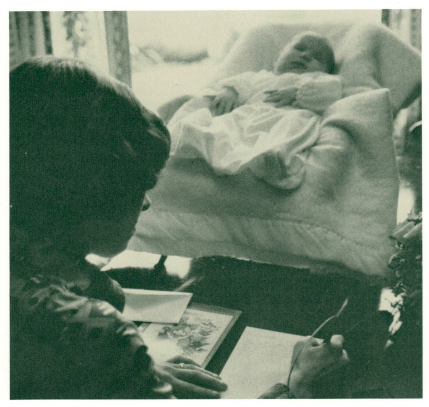

"I wrote this," she told me, "when you had neither ruffles nor curls. I've saved it for you until you were old enough to understand. I hope you can know the love contained in this envelope."

I sat up, took the letter, and she left me. I opened the envelope carefully and unfolded the pages.

My daughter:

You finally arrived! How I have longed for a little girl of my own! But now that you are here, I find myself a bit frightened. What shall I do with you? There will be dresses to make, curls to keep, femininity to develop, boundaries to set, morals to instill. Can I be a good mother to a girl?

I want to try.

Your hair is black and straight; your eyes are blue. You are lying in your pink-trimmed basket blowing shimmering bubbles of saliva through your parted lips. I have a daughter! *My* daughter. Not reasoning why, I sit here looking at you, wondering in disbelief when I shall awaken from my dream to find you belong to someone else.

My daughter—I watch you now in the dawn of your life—marveling over the miniature yawns, tiny wet sneezes, tremulously smiling lips, the grasping fist tightening about my finger—and feel the weight of my responsibility to guide your life as you grow "in wisdom and stature and in favor with God and man."

This morning, I resolve to deepen my spiritual life. I need to be closer to God since I am now the mother of a daughter.

I resolve to spend more time in prayer, striving toward the high ideal of praying without ceasing. I do not want my prayer life to be merely a habit, but instead that all through the day I will feel God's presence with me, and prayer will be a spontaneous outburst of my heart.

I resolve to read my Bible daily. Within its pages I will find the key to a closer walk with God and to the frustrations of life. Whether it be a verse or several chapters, I want to read until I find a personal message for me that day.

I resolve to make a habit of "giving thanks in all things." Instead of spending too much of my time and energies on the disappointments and sorrows of life, I will cultivate the radiance that comes from concentrating on the good and happy things. I want to show forth the "joy of the Lord" in all of the routine of life.

I resolve to develop a Christian atmosphere in the home in which my daughter will grow. This will include my attitude toward people, my conversations, and my everyday dealings with neighbors and friends.

I resolve to spend time with my daughter in play and, as she grows older, to establish a real bond of fellowship that will help me to understand her heart and mind so that I may better influence her for right.

I resolve to live with the knowledge ever before me that the actions I take, the words I speak, and the places I go will be the same actions my daughter will want to imitate, the words my daughter first will lisp, and the places where my footsteps will lead her. I will live so that when she is grown, she will have a vital personal relationship with God.

I resolve regularly to attend the services in our church. I wish to set an example for my daughter that I will want her to follow throughout the years of her life.

I resolve not to wreak the frustrations of the day upon my child. I want her to remember my voice as sweet and kind.

I resolve to cultivate tolerance and love in such dimensions that I will not give in to angry, thoughtless reprimands that could cut their cruel way across the happiness of my family. I will not become so self-absorbed or anxious over problems that I forget or ignore my daughter's need of me as a mother. I must earn the right to mold her life.

I have a daughter. My daughter.

My never-to-die daughter now lying in a pink-trimmed basket is blissfully unaware of the eternal nature of her soul. But I am both aware and concerned with her immortality, for I realize that, in great measure, her destiny depends on me.

> My daughter:
> You are so young;
> And I who love you so
> Am held responsible
> That you may know God's love.
>
> You are so small;
> And I, myself, so weak,
> Must lead you to my Christ
> Before you seek
> Another way.
>
> Your little life
> Is in my keeping here;
> God grant me wisdom, grace,
> And godly fear,
> I pray.*

Truly it is an awesome time: A TIME TO BE BORN . . . a Mother!

*Author Unknown

A Time to Plant

Horace Bushnell, a nineteenth-century theologian, once said: "Let every Christian father and mother understand when the child is three years old that they have done more than half they ever will do for his character."

My mother penned this statement on the flyleaf of her diary and lived in the belief that its truth impelled her to "plant" from earliest infancy. As soon as we children were born, we spent our lives in an atmosphere saturated with lullabies about God, prayers to God, and services about God.

I heard my mother say often, "Training my children is the most important task I have while they are under my care, and nothing shall interfere with that training. The housework, social obligations—all must be subservient to the welfare of my children." And this she practiced.

Everyday in the summertime, she would load us into the little red wagon and take us out under some large tree. There she would tell us Bible stories, illustrating them in sand, with rocks and stones for houses and mountains, and using twigs to represent the patriarchs of old.

When it was too cold for the red wagon excursions, she would gather us about her in front of the fire. There, in the soft warm light, by which men have dreamed since they first learned to rub dry sticks

together for a spark, she showed us pictures and told us stories. In this manner she captured our imaginations, and our heroes became Daniel, Stephen, and Rhoda instead of Errol Flynn, Charles Atlas, and Marilyn Monroe.

We were taught to recite Scriptures and to pray before we could intelligibly say much else. Before we started school, we could recite the books of the Bible in order, name the twelve disciples, and quote more Scripture than many preachers.

I will never forget the thrill I had when, at the age of five years, I outquoted my brother, who was a senior in high school, in a Scripture recitation contest. We grew up with the Word of God as a very real part of our lives.

Mother wrote in her diary: "The sculptor spends hours in shaping the features of the face; the painter labors to give color to the hair or expression to the face. Their work is to stand for ages to come.

"I, as a mother, am shaping substances more imperishable than canvas or marble. I can afford to be patient and wait long for results. I have eternity in which to watch developments."

Mother worked patiently and consistently. When we grew older, she would pick out chapters and portions of Scripture, and give us a bundle of magazines, scissors, glue, and a scrapbook of some sort. Then she would challenge us to illustrate the chapter with pictures out of the magazines. Needless to say, we loved every minute of it and memorized those chapters word for word.

Mother played Bible games of all types with us. If we ran out of games, she dreamed up new ones. She could always be counted on for companionship, fun, and—though sometimes not blatantly obvious—religious training.

Whether she was cooking, ironing, rolling my

hair in curlers, or just talking, Mother impressed upon us that neither valor nor riches nor the wisdom of all the sages could ever suffice our souls—that only through living for Christ could we find complete fulfillment and the beauty of dreams come true.

She told us Bible stories and then challenged us to live like their heroes. We could listen to the story of the patience of Job, the sweet spirit of Joseph, and dream within ourselves that "some day" we would be like that. She knew that our dreams of service must have an outlet if anything was to be realized from them.

In her personal scrapbook, she penned these words:

Every child is a bundle of tremendous possibilities; and whether the child shall come forth to life, its heart attuned to the eternal harmonies, and after a life of usefulness on earth go to a life of joy in heaven, or whether across it shall be etched with eternal discord, and after a life of wrongdoing on earth it shall go to a home of impenetrable darkness, is being decided now by a nursery song, Bible story, an evening prayer, a walk, a ride, a look, a frown, and a smile.

My job as a mother is so vital that it demands my highest skills and finest talents.

"I can do now with a touch as light as a feather what I cannot later accomplish with the pressure of a hundredweight."—Froebel.

Truly it is a demanding time, A TIME TO PLANT!

A Time to Love

The one emotional food that every human being needs is love, and a person can never receive too much. There can be an overabundance of discipline, an excess of independence, but the more love one receives the better.

Mother became upset with one of my cousins whose baby was crying in its crib. The baby was obviously unhappy, and so was the mother who paced the floor, saying, "He isn't sick; he isn't hungry; he isn't wet. Why won't he quit crying?"

Mother said: "Maybe he's hungry emotionally. Maybe he needs your love."

"But it isn't time for me to pick him up," my book-following cousin cried.

Mother scoffed.

"He can't read the clock. He only knows that within him it is time for love. Give it to him."

Finally, my cousin picked up the baby, and she and the infant both sighed with relief. I read recently that "letting the baby cry is psychologically harmful to both mother and child." Love is the binding force between all human beings, but especially is love imperative between mother and child. And the more love is shown, the happier for all concerned.

From the moment of birth on is a time for love between mother and child. Not only may love be demonstrated physically but also in many other ways.

When I was five, I wanted to help my mother prepare for company. Without her knowledge I took a rag and a small pail of water to a front window and scrubbed away. When Mother came in later and saw my streaked effort, she said: "Thank you! I needed that window washed badly."

I shrugged grandly. "It was nothing," I said.

But it *was* something to me—and I knew her love.

Another time I presented her a crayoned masterpiece on red construction paper. Proudly I told her that I had "painted" the picture to go over the sofa in the living room. She graciously enthused over my idea and put it over the sofa, under the large picture already there and told me she liked mine the best.

She left it there for several days and proudly pointed it out to her friends. Nor did she excuse it as "little daughter's drawing." She gave it dignity by its position and her comments, and thus conferred the precious gift of self-esteem to my young and vulnerable heart—and I knew her love.

I remember when I ran across two forbidden streets to the home of one of my playmates. When Mother found me, she marched me home and administered a sound spanking. After that bit of business was cared for, she took me in her arms, caressed my heaving shoulders, and assured me she loved me.

She explained it was because of her love that she bothered to discipline me, a concept my childish mind readily perceived. That night when I knelt by my bed to pray, I said: "O God, thank You that Mother spanked me to goodness today—and may the goodness last the rest of my life."

I don't recall the prayer, but my mother

laughingly told it for years. I do remember her discipline. Somehow she convinced me she was disapproving of my actions, not of me, and in that distinction, I knew her love.

The night of the P.T.A. exhibition, I was scheduled to show my talent in two events: singing and pole vaulting. It turned out to be a catastrophe.

When Lou Ellen and I went to sing our duet, we got tickled and laughed all the way through the song. When I went rushing out to vault the pole, set at about two feet, I hit the pole and collapsed in a jumble of bony legs, flying pigtails, and screams.

When the program was over, Mother came to me and asked me to come and meet one of her friends. With obvious pride, she presented me, and I looked up at her in astonishment. She had no earthly reason to even admit I was hers, but her eyes touched me tenderly, and her praises of my few accomplishments were sincere—and I knew her love.

Loving a child doesn't mean pampering him. It doesn't mean buying him every toy in the stores' windows. Loving a child is saying through word and deed, "I love you not for what you do—or for what you don't do. I love you just because you're you." This is the uncritical kind of love demanded of a mother in the never-ending TIME TO LOVE!

A Time to Keep

"Heart Talk," she called it.

These were times when we could talk freely about any and all topics. She worked for those times, crowding them into schedules so chock full of other things there would seem to be no time for a little girl. But she harnessed times of dish washing, hair curling, berry picking, jam canning into "heart talk" sessions when necessary. But the best times were those when Daddy was still at the office, and all of the other children were away. Then we would curl up on her bed and have real "heart talks."

I remember well the night I asked her where I could find God. As a juvenile realist, I was searching for a person whom I could see and touch. When I informed her of the futility of my search, she laughed and opened her Bible to the picture of the children gathered about Christ.

"Here," she said. "We find God best in the life of Christ." And then she told me of the Galilean and the coming of the children to Him. I had heard it a thousand times, but it took on new meaning that night. Mother helped me to feel the love of Christ, His tenderness, His concern.

I felt that I was a part of that group of children. I imagined that it was I pushing up to His knee.

"I found a bird's nest today," I told Him.

The Lord's eyes shone with interest. "Did it have eggs in it?"

I nodded importantly. "Yes, they were china blue. Very tiny—about the size of a sling-shot stone."

Mother made Jesus live for me. If I could find God in His life, then I could give my love to Him wholeheartedly.

One time (so my mother tells me) I caught her off balance. As soon as we curled up on the bed, I innocently cast my bombshell. "Mother, Dorry said her mother is going to have a baby. Dorry told me all about how it happens."

Mother hadn't planned to discuss sex with me at this early age. But since I was interested, she valiantly tried to readjust her time schedule to fit mine. She quietly allowed me to tell her all that Dorry had to say. Then she corrected some mistaken ideas and explained things further.

When my curiosity was satisfied, I dropped the subject and went on to other important matters, such as the color of drapes I should choose for my doll house.

On a 1948 cover of the *Saturday Evening Post*, Norman Rockwell depicted a husband holding a paper with a picture of Dewey, while his wife held tenaciously to one with a picture of Truman. They were angrily screaming at each other while the dog crouched under the chair, and their little boy cried with fright because the stability of his life was threatened.

My parents never screamed angrily at each other. However, I clearly remember times when there was cold silence between them. I found this as terrifying and upsetting as the little boy in Rockwell's picture found his parents' political melee.

Only after the coldness had vanished and things

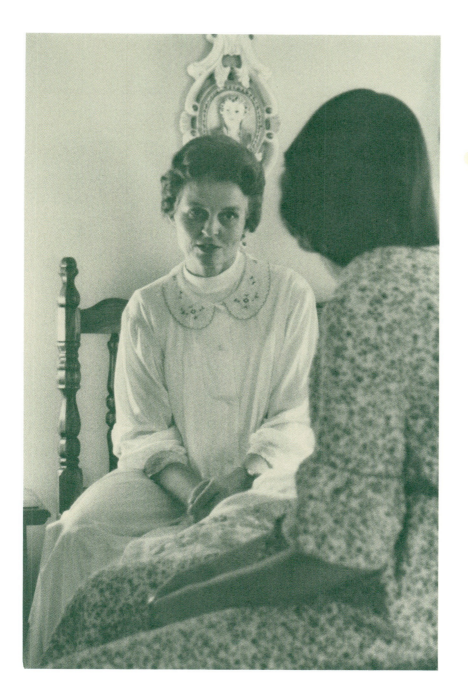

were back on an even keel did we discuss it in "Heart Talk." When I told Mother of my disturbance, her eyes filled with tears.

She talked long about the differences between her background and my father's. She explained the loving, sharing relationship of her family as opposed to my father's stern, inarticulate father who reared his children alone after the death of his wife.

This diversity in backgrounds caused many disagreements between my parents in their concepts of life in general. She talked about how hard they both had tried—and were trying—to understand each other.

And then she would say something comforting, "Just remember that down underneath the surface, in the depths of each of our hearts, there is love and trust and loyalty, strong and unalterable. You can always believe in that."

I could understand occasional quarrels, and I found security in my mother's admission of their changeless love in spite of their humanity.

Vitally important in the lives of children is the moment when they understand the humanity of their parents, for then they respect them more and are encouraged to believe that, despite their own humanity, they might some day be as great.

Aldous Huxley said in *Do What You Will!:*

> To aspire to be superhuman is a most discreditable admission that you lack the guts, the wit, the moderating judgment to be successfully and consummately human.

What better time for confession of parents' fallibility than in "Heart Talk?" What better time to hold a child near? What more precious time than A TIME TO KEEP?

A Time to Cast Away

Childhood is a time filled with challenges that are accompanied by fear and anxiety. It takes great courage to learn about life and to grow up.

Because my father was a minister, we moved every three or four years. When I was eight, we moved to a town in western Texas. I felt strange and ill at ease. When the time came to go to school that first day, there was a large lump in my stomach that kept moving ominously about, threatening to jump out of my constricted throat.

Mother helped me dress in my blue jumper, and just as she was finishing the braids of my hair, I reached my limit. I jumped away, ran to my strange new bedroom, threw myself on the familiar bed and began to sob: "I can't! I can't! I can't! I *can't!*"

Mother followed me into the bedroom. She pulled me to my feet and said very firmly: "Yes, you can. Now let's get this hair finished."

But I whirled away. "Mother, I'm afraid. I don't know *anybody*. I can't! I *can't!*"

Mother led me to a chair and began smoothing my rumpled hair. "I don't ever want to hear you say that phrase again. You *can* do whatever you have to do. Life is not easy, but neither is it unconquerable. You *can* do whatever is set before you."

She gave my hair a few finishing brush strokes, and then she started for the door. Sullenly I arose and walked after her. When we got to the porch, she looked at me searchingly: "You can, can't you?"

I nodded. "I'll try," I muttered.

"That's all I ask," she said quietly as I went down the walk.

We repeated that incident on numerous occasions with various terrifying causes. One time I was called upon to play the piano for a school program. At the last minute, I flew into a panic of fear.

"I can't! I can't!"

"That is the phrase you are forbidden to use," she said unnecessarily. I knew that, but in my terror, I cared little.

"But Mother, I can't! You know I never get that one arpeggio right."

"I will hear no more," she said with determination. "You can do your best. You have not been asked to present a perfect performance. You have only been asked to do your best. And if that includes a faulty arpeggio, so be it. But you *can* perform. You *can* do whatever is set before you."

And I did. And I muffed the arpeggio just as I had predicted I would.

But although I wanted to be crushed about the errant notes, my mother kept insisting I had done my best. *My* best! Perhaps someone else could have done it perfectly. At age ten, with *my* particular training and ability, it had been out of my reach. But I had only been asked to do *my* best. That I had done; it was good enough.

As I look back, I realize my mother was exerting caution in helping me set goals. If they were too high, I would become discouraged; if too low, I would not be challenged. And she did want to dare me always to do my best, whatever that best might be.

In childhood, the world seems vast and alien and

impersonal. Only when these fears are cast away by a perceptive mother can the child emerge to face maturity with courage. He should be challenged to drop the words "I can't" from his vocabulary and to substitute a will to try.

Then, most importantly, he should be helped to accept himself just as he is. He should be able to look at his weaknesses and deficiencies without flinching or apologizing. He must be made to know that he does not have to stand at the top of the ladder in order to feel achievement. The need of a child to learn self-acceptance points up the wise and loving skill asked of a mother at A TIME TO CAST AWAY.

A Time to Gather Stones Together

She was perched on a stepladder, engrossed in arranging a set of blue dishes in the top cabinet, when the kitchen door burst open and two small children bounded into the room.

"Mommy! Mommy! Come quick! We've just found the *biggest black bug*!"

The two pairs of blue eyes were dancing gaily; the words tumbled from rosy lips. The taller girl held her palms closely clamped together holding the "biggest black bug" in captivity.

The habitual, angry reprimand rose to the lips of the mother, but on a sudden impulse she paused a moment, considering. Why not stop and see the black bug? Why not share a discovery with the children?

In this frame of mind, Pam climbed down from the stepladder to investigate the big, black bug held firmly in the damp, chubby palms of the little girl. Truly it was a big, black bug—one that even Pam had never seen before. Intrigued, she went to the encyclopedia and looked it up. There followed a fascinating half hour as the two little girls and Mommy learned all of the vital things about the "biggest black bug!"

When she got back to arranging dishes, Pam considered the experience with the bug. She had always, just always, impatiently declined any such notions before; but after accepting this invitation to explore and learn with her children, she realized she

43

hadn't lost any more time than if she had been on the telephone with her sister. And she had done something important and constructive with her children. Perhaps, she mused thoughtfully, I ought to change my immediate reactions to the children's pleas from an automatic "no" to the question, "Why not?" And if the answer brings nothing wrong or dangerous, then I could enjoy a new experience in learning with them.

My friend's decision at this point reminded me of my mother who must have made a similar decision, for she was always ready to enter a new door of delight.

One night, I queried, "Mother, what are those bobbing lights?"

She answered hurriedly in the midst of her work. "Those are lightning bugs. I used to catch them when I was a little girl."

"Oh Mother, can I? Can I?"

She looked wistfully at the work that needed doing, and then she smiled and said, "Why not?"

And then forgetting the work, she grabbed a quart jar and proceeded into the lavender-scented outdoors to feel, with her child, the thrill of racing through the warm air to catch lightning bugs.

I remember one night as we were finishing supper, my daddy told a boyhood tale of how he and his cousin used to make the bullfrogs sing bass to an old song. Immediately I began to ask if we could go to Myers Creek where Johnny Crathord said bullfrogs sang.

"Could we? Please, can't we go and hear the bullfrogs sing with Daddy? Please—huh—please!"

Mother smiled. "Why not?"

And so we got into the car and went to Myers Creek. We crept down to the water situating ourselves very quietly. I was nearly bursting with excitement. Then, in his deep bass voice, Daddy began his old song.

After the first stanza, he motioned for Mother and me to join in. We did and sang lustily for a few stanzas, listening intently for the bass of the bullfrog. Then we heard it!

Down deep in the reeds at our left, we heard it—the deep bass, rumbling refrain of the bullfrog.

In a moment another began, then another, then another.

Awe, thrill, and delight filled my entire body.

It was a family experience I shall never forget. I learned about bullfrogs that night—but something much greater than that also. I learned of family unity, family togetherness, and family sharing in the beauty of God's creation.

The work neglected to chase lightning bugs, the dishes belatedly put on the shelf to investigate a big black bug, the table left uncleared at home when a family sang songs with bullfrogs are of little consequence to the mother who truly understands the importance of making children secure in family experiences . . . the mother who is careful to house her child in a haven of love, the mother who understands A TIME TO GATHER STONES TOGETHER.

A Time to Mourn

It was my first confrontation with death.

My tall, silver-haired grandfather had fallen; his hip was broken. After surgery, he never regained consciousness.

We all went to Fort Worth, Texas. Uncle Joe sat on the back steps, ill with grief. Mother and her sisters and brother wept copiously. Grandmother was bent with pain. Sober-looking cousins, whom I had never seen before, stood about.

In my life span, we had never lived near my grandparents; therefore I only knew my grandfather briefly. This was not a time of personal loss for me. But I was deeply concerned for my brothers, who knew him better, and especially worried for my mother, whose suffering was deep.

On the day of the funeral my spirits were heavy. I listened to the intoning of the minister, the singing of the songs. I watched Mother and wondered if she would ever smile again.

When my parents walked beside the coffin for the last time, I saw my father's hands tremble. I observed the deep sadness on Mother's face, as if it were engraved there for all time.

I stood briefly beside the coffin and searched my grandfather's still face for some answer to the dilemma of death. There was no message.

I cried.

When we returned home, life moved on.

I still lived in the same house, consumed cornbread and peach cobbler, and played with my dolls. Mother cared for the house in her usual manner, cooked our meals, and made my dolls new clothes—but she was different. There was an air of abstraction about her. I never knew for sure whether she really saw me, or whether she simply responded to my needs from reflex.

I remember standing at the kitchen window late one evening. The sun had been pushed from the sky by the muscled arms of darkness. It seemed as if those muscled arms were tatooed with the word "never." My grandfather would *never* return. Life would *never* be the same.

Mother was busily at work. But I knew tears were spilling into the cake batter.

Still looking out the window I said, "Mother, isn't Grandfather in heaven?"

"Of course," she assured me, "Of course."

My brows were knit.

"Then why do you cry?"

She came to me quickly.

"I cry not for him, but for me. You see, life will never be the same for me since he is gone, and the pain of adjustment makes me cry."

She turned me toward her. Her face was strained. "Can you understand that?"

I knew she was concerned that she might be damaging my faith in life after death.

I nodded slowly.

Then I remembered something.

"Jesus wept," I said.

She pulled me to her in relief. "What a lovely thing to say! You do understand? We should not take lightly an event that caused even Jesus to weep."

I have since learned that the way one looks at

death colors the manner in which one responds to life. Regardless of our concept of death's being a door to immortality, and the grandeur of such a hope, the human part of grief is a real fact of life. Wise is the mother who does not try to shield her children from observing, even knowing grief, but instead helps the child to know that in every life, there comes a justified TIME TO MOURN.

50 *A Time to Cast Away Stones*

"Johnny, if you get out of this car again, I will spank you!"

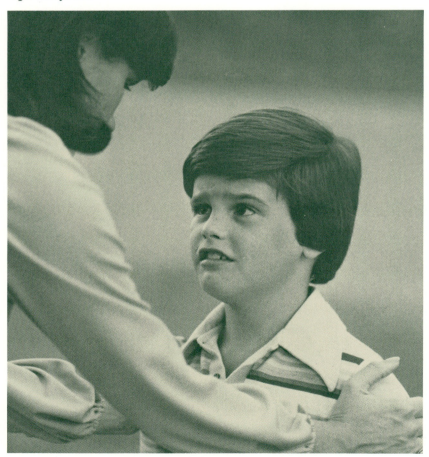

The car door was closed upon the small culprit, and his mother returned to talk with my mother who was waiting for her at the front of the car. After a moment's pause, the car door opened and Johnny jumped out, running for the stone steps of the nearby church.

Spying him, his mother ran after him. Grabbing him up, she again deposited him inside the car, threatening, "I mean it, young man. If you do that again, I will spank you."

Returning to talk with my mother, she had hardly picked up the conversational threads when the door opened, and Johnny dashed up the stone steps of the church. His mother raced after him, uttering threats, which she and my mother—and the child as well—knew she had not the slightest intention of carrying out.

Commenting upon this incident later, Mother said she felt one of the greatest weaknesses in the homes of today is that so many parents lie to their children. This is a startling accusation and one from which we want to shrink, crying, "Not guilty!"

But let us consider it for a moment. We as parents are the ones who teach our children either to respect or to ignore what is right or lawful. This important area of our children's development is dependent upon our truthfulness and faithfulness in this respect.

If we make laws the children may break at will, they will not understand later why they should respect the laws of God and country. If we make promises that are never carried out, our children will not come to believe in the word of state or in divine commandment.

A parent should never commit himself on a point unless he intends to carry it out to the letter. If you do not intend to punish Johnny for getting out of the car, then don't say you will. Don't lie to your child!

It has been said, "The most difficult career in the

world has been given to amateurs: parenthood." While most parents are vaguely conscious of the awesomeness of their responsibility, they may go through the early years of a child's life failing to teach the greatest lesson the child must learn.

Parenthood is filled with many duties and responsibilities, but parents must never become too busy to see that the child learns the most important lesson in life—obedience. When a command is given, it should be inbred from infancy that it is to be obeyed.

The child's most important period of development is his first three years, for it is here that his personality and future habit-patterns are set. During this time he collides with the word "no" and the moral ideas of "must" and "must not," and he decides what he will do with them. It is up to the parent to determine whether that decision will be respect or contempt.

A teen-age girl wept in my home recently. She had come seeking spiritual help. She would try to pray and then would stop, dissolving in tears. Finally, in desperation she looked up at me and said: "If I become a Christian, I would have to obey God—and I have never had to obey anyone in my life!"

She knew God's Word was true.

His promises were real, and this was an unfamiliar area to her.

Only the week before I had been in her home. Her mother had told her to hang up her coat and put away the scattered schoolbooks, but the girl had gone blissfully on with a novel she was reading. Her mother said, "If you don't mind me, you will not go to the party tonight."

But the teen-ager was oblivious to the command and the threat, for she knew —just as I knew—her mother was not being honest. When I left their home, the coat and books were still on the couch, and the girl went to the party that night. Her mother's commands were idle; her threats, untrue.

Now the girl was faced with a spiritual crisis and she could not find peace, for she had never learned the lesson of obedience.

There is a difference between discipline and punishment. Punishment means hurting someone, paying him back for a wrong. Discipline, on the other hand, suggests an action directed toward a specific goal. You discipline to assist the recipient in self-improvement.

The basic rule of discipline is to establish yourself as authority. Be consistent in your use of that authority, and direct all criticism at the act instead of at the child. The conscientious mother must take time, energy, patience, will, and perseverance in an effort to help her children—A TIME TO CAST AWAY STONES.

A Time to Heal

I hid in the closet.

The Sunday school superintendent had told me he would let me pick up the Sunday school books from the classes. The regular secretary was gone and he was planning to do her work. I could help.

Thrilled at the prospect, I counted the days for the rest of the week. I was going to have the "glory" of picking up Sunday school books!

But when Sunday came, an older girl was asked to do the entire job in the regular secretary's absence. My dreams of glory were shattered.

I sat through Sunday school in sullen anguish. As soon as the bell rang, I ran to our parsonage next door and hid in the closet.

There I cried and whispered to myself the dire dimensions of my injuries. I dredged through all of my life for other wounds. The total was staggering.

When Mother missed me in the church service, she came looking and found me in the closet.

She looked at my tear-swollen face and sighed. She was under pressure. People would whisper about the minister's wife not being in church, but she could tell I was going to take some time.

"What is the matter?" she asked with resignation.

I explained my utter rejection by the Sunday school superintendent who had *promised!*

"He found a girl who could do the entire job,"

Mother explained. "He didn't remember his
promise to you."

"Well, he should have!" I exploded.
"Aren't I a person?"

"Yes, you're a person," she said slowly. "A
person who can give as well as receive."

"How does that fit in here?" I demanded.

Her eyes began to sparkle, and I knew she had

finally decided what to do about me. She left the room and returned with a tablet and pencil.

"Ruth, I know you are hurt. But life will bring you many times of pain caused by the thoughtlessness of others. So now is the time to begin thinking about focus."

"Focus? What are you talking about?"

"Focus means to turn and center your attention on something. In times when you are disappointed, let down by people, by life—to what do you turn your attention? Upon your one loss, or upon all of your gifts?

"I don't understand," I said. "I only understand that he promised and . . ."

She handed me the tablet and pencil.

"I want you to see if you can understand what I am talking about. Instead of placing your attention on this one broken promise that has brought you pain, try to turn it upon your whole life and all the gifts you have received.

"List them all here. And when you are through, if you still feel justified in crying over this disappointment, I want you to stay home from church and cry all morning. If you do not feel justified, you may join us in church whenever you are ready."

"But I don't understand!" I cried.

"Work on it," she said and left me.

I sat there, chewing thoughtfully on the pencil.

"Focus," she had said.

That's what Daddy said when he was putting the spotlight on something he wanted to see at night.

Mother wants me to quit spotlighting this broken promise long enough to spotlight my whole life of gifts. Well, that won't be very many!

Not only had the Sunday school superintendent broken his promise, but Rhonda had promised to give me a blue doll dress, and she hadn't. And Daddy had promised we would go on a picnic, but he had a hospital call he went to instead.

The list was endless. I was certain I was, of all people, the most mistreated, the most unloved. So it surely wouldn't hurt to go along with Mother's game in order to please her. Then I could cry the rest of the morning.

I wrote at the top of the page, "My Gifts." Then I listed them:

> *Doll with the blue eyes*
> *Golden-brown teddy bear*
> *Basketball*

My list had begun with *things*.
Soon it progressed to *people*:

> *Daddy*
> *Mother*
> *Lyman*
> *Joe*
> *Elton*
> *Aunt Euna*

Then it moved to *intangibles*:

> *Laughter*
> *Security*
> *Love*
> *Beauty*
> *God*

Beginning with the small, everyday things of my world, my list spiraled higher until my thoughts were hurled in gratitude to God Himself.

I looked at the filled sheets of paper. My eyes were blurred with tears. Not tears of self-pity. Tears of thanksgiving.

     I climbed out of the closet. I was ready to go to church. ''Focus'' was the medicine my mother prescribed to heal my pain over a broken promise. I found it did bring healing—not only that day in the closet, but in larger disappointments, more painful wounds all through life.

     Norman Vincent Peale would call it the power of positive thinking. Psychologists would call it auto-suggestion. In terms my childish mind could understand, my mother called it focus. And its magic healed my pain.

     How wise a mother to know the right prescription when she becomes the physician IN A TIME TO HEAL.

A Time to Build Up

"Thank you very much for coming," Anne smiled graciously at the buxom lady who was bustling out of the door. "It was nice meeting you, and I will plan to attend the book review if at all possible."

The door closed behind the visitor. Anne hurried to the picture over the piano and straightened it. She had noticed it was awry while her visitor was talking.

"Mommy," came a childish treble behind her.

Frowning, Anne turned and asked crossly, "What do you want?"

Becky stood there in all her six-year-old smallness and studied her mother seriously. Then she said, "Mommy, you must love Mrs. Johnson better'n me!"

Anne stared at the child in disbelief. Incredulously she asked, "Whatever makes you say that?"

"Well, you're nicer to her'n you are to me! You hollered at me before she came, but you talked sweet to her. And as soon as she left, you frowned at me. But you smiled at her! So you must love Mrs. Johnson better'n me."

At that moment, Susan came to the door and called Becky outside to ride bicycles. Becky ran in childish eagerness out the door, forgetting her somber mood. But her mother stood still in the middle of the floor.

"Why, she's right," she said to herself in

consternation. "She's right! I am nice and polite to an utter stranger, but for the ones I love the very best, I have only frowns and bitter tones."

"That's all wrong," she mused, as she started toward the kitchen, where a bell announced that her roast was done. "It just isn't fair for me to give my best—my charm, my courtesy, my understanding—to those whom I barely know, and reserve my worst—my hollering, my frowns, my impatience—for those who are the dearest in all the world!

Anne took the roast from the oven as her husband came through the door, sniffing the air. He tossed his briefcase on the kitchen table. Anne went to him, took off his hat, kissed his cheek, and said: "Hi, Darling. Welcome home."

Jim held her at arm's length, staring at her in amazement. He touched her head playfully.

"No fever," he announced, acting relieved. "But something is wrong somewhere. You usually don't have time even to say 'Hi!' much less a real greeting like this. What happened?"

"Oh, nothing," Anne teased. "I just decided to treat you like a stranger."

"A stranger?"

It was Jim's turn at incredulity. "I hope you don't kiss every stranger who enters your door."

Anne laughed. "No, not that. But I do smile and treat them with courtesy and kindness, and that is a lot more than I usually do for my family. So . . . I've decided to change. As of now, I am resolving to be as nice to those whom I love as I am to casual friends."

"Sounds good to me," Jim said as he tasted the roast. He licked his fingers. "Tell you what. I'll join you. We will make a pact to be as kind to each other—and to our children—as we are to strangers. Is it a deal?" He tilted her face.

"It's a deal," she responded earnestly.

When my friend told me of her pact with her husband, my eyes suddenly filled with tears. I could remember my mother, standing in the middle of the kitchen floor, looking thoughtfully at a little girl.

"I've had choir practice, weekday Bible school, missionary meeting, and squeezed in three hospital calls today. If my nerves are on edge, forgive me."

Then she would grin and I would quote along with her:

> We have sweet smiles for the stranger,
>   Kind words for the sometimes guest;
> But oft' for our own the bitter tone,
>   Though we love our own the best!

Then we would laugh.

A million times, I have heard her quote that quatrain to herself or to me. From my vantage point, I could not see its necessity to her. I understood it only as her philosophy. But as I look back, I know she was quoting it to remind herself to hold steady under pressure, to refrain from wreaking jagged nerves on her child.

And it must have always worked its magic. I have no memories of her bitter tone. Her smiles dominated my life.

Restraint, discipline, and control extend sweetness and love to the child a mother "loves the best" when she is aware of her responsibility in A TIME TO BUILD UP.

A Time to Weep

I remember finding Mother's tears on my toast.

I got up and went to the cabinet where she was working. And I saw the salty cascade on her cheeks.

She turned when she saw me and took me in her arms. She buried her head on my shoulder, and we both shook from the impact of her sobs. My hands stroked her hair as my mind puzzled over the reason.

When she finally gained control, she told me about Pearl Harbor. The Japanese had attacked; our nation was at war.

The tears began again as she said, "I never thought I would live to see the day when another generation of young men would have to go to war. And among them my son."

She pulled me to her again. Her tears soaked my dress. Soon mine mingled with hers. I had finally figured out that war was bad. War would take away my brother.

So it was early in my life that Mother taught me the dignity and value of tears. Although she showed remarkable restraint in most areas of life, Mother strongly believed in weeping.

"Jesus wept," she reminded me at these times. "When the heart is in deep agony, tears are God's finest medicine. We are foolish when we do not use them."

But there was more to her philosophy of weeping.

"Tears in private give you courage in public," was one of her self-made axioms. And this was her practice.

When the day finally came and my tall, good-looking brother had to go away to war, her privately shed tears gave her the courage to smile during her farewell. But I was too young for that kind of courage. My tears dampened everyone about me, and when we returned home, I flung myself across the bed in a sobbing six-year-old heap.

My father came and sat beside me, stroking my hot forehead and dampened curls. Finally, his voice reached me. "Don't cry, Honey. He is in God's hands, and God's hands are big enough to hold him."

I latched onto that statement of faith.

Soon I could go wash my face and resume the process of living. But it wasn't easy. At first my parents and I cried during family prayers because Joe was not there to kneel with us.

Sunday came.

Joe was gone.

The lump in my throat was larger than a gum ball. I couldn't get it to budge in any direction.

I dressed in the blue dress Joe had always liked. He had called me Ollie, which I furiously resented (yet secretly loved), and had teased me that the blue dress would surely make the boys' hearts flutter.

When I was ready to go to church, I saw Mother watching me. Her face was smiling; only her eyes told of tears.

I tried to swallow the lump again. It would not move.

So taking a deep breath, I walked out the door without saying a word. All the time I felt like two people, one wanting to run back, the other marching straight ahead with shoulders back and chin up—the way Mother wanted me to look when I had to step off into something taking a great deal of courage.

"Tears are God's finest medicine."

"Tears in private give you courage in public."

What important lessons to instill in the hearts of children as they face life! There is healing; there is courage in A TIME TO WEEP.

66 A Time to Dance

THIS IS THE DAY THE LORD HATH MADE!
What triumph and pure ecstasy Mother put into
those words when she came to waken me from sleep. I
was not impressed with His handiwork at that moment.
But Mother's joy ultimately dispelled my early-morning
glumness until I, too, noticed the fragrant air, the
skipping sunbeams, the flitting blue jays and was glad.

Mother was convinced that little girls needed lots
of play, and in the process of that play, she opened
doors of her heart that otherwise never would have been
opened. In retrospect, I understand the price Mother
paid to play with me. At the time, I thought she did it
because it was fun. But Mother was wise enough to
know that if she had time to play with me, I would have
time to pray with her.

Mother played Ping-Pong with me in the
basement. It was a game I could never conquer. If I
managed to hit the tiny ball with the paddle, I walloped
it into the next room, if it found the door. If it did not, it
ricocheted off the wall. I was always convinced I
would be a champion with my powerful swing, but my
conviction has never proven much.

No one has ever played more than one game of
Ping-Pong with me except my mother. But she was
always ready. And I remember happy hours spent with
her at the Ping-Pong table. Because of my ineptitude at
the game and the fact that she was forty-three years old

at my birth, which made her major days of Ping-Pong playing at age fifty-three to fifty-six, I doubt her memories contained much fun!

Mother played basketball with me and rejoiced over my "terrific" accuracy at hitting the basket. She played baseball with me and could hit a baseball farther than I ever could.

She was always game for a picnic, and often we hiked out to the location. Sometimes we raced part of the way, and because she was a minister's wife, this caused much headshaking among some people who did not understand her "lack of dignity." But Mother would laugh and say, "If David could dance before the Lord, I guess He won't mind our racing," and off she would run, with me following close behind her. Her willingness to "race before the Lord" in spite of people's disdain made me open my heart even wider to a God who enjoyed dancing and running!

When things began to be too humdrum, Mother would look for a "joy shock," something beautiful to break through the gray window of boredom. At this, she was a genius.

I remember her saying to my father one afternoon, as he was leaving for his office, that she felt he should not go. He looked at her in astonishment and she, in turn, looked meaningfully at me sitting disconsolately with my paper dolls.

Then my mother announced that next Sunday's sermon would "keep" long enough for the three of us to go fly a kite. *Go fly a kite!* I had seen big kids do it, but I had never been invited to try. My squeal of delight at being given the opportunity to do something I had dreamed about, but certainly did not expect, was of such dimension that my father quickly agreed to postpone the sermon.

Down to the store we went for a kite, then out to

the country where we proceeded to make the long tail out of rags from Mother's rag drawer. All the time, I was talking a mile a minute from sheer delight.

When we finally got the giant kite into the air, my father let me hold the ball of twine. I ran in crazy circles, watching the kite repeat my wild antics in the sky. The tug in my hand was exhilarating, and I was filled with happiness.

Mother and Daddy both took turns executing sky dances with the kite. Time slipped by, and all of us were unaware.

As the youngest of eight children, by many years, I was alone at home with my parents most of my life. There were no siblings to play with, to plot with, to dance with. Many moments would have deteriorated into monotony for a little child alone in a parsonage had not concerned parents been wise enough to understand the value of "joy shocks."

Later, in a class at the university I attended, I was asked to give my first impressions to certain words. When the word "happiness" was stated, I immediately responded, "kite flying." The listening group was surprised, and so was I, for I had not consciously thought of the childhood incident in years. But in a special sense, it had remained with me. I will always understand happiness in terms begun in a moment when my parents abandoned duties to fly a kite.

Balanced meals, galoshes on rainy days, homework in the evening, teeth braces, piano lessons—all are a part of the responsibility of a good mother. Of no less importance is her willingness to shed dignity and other duties in A TIME TO DANCE.

A Time to Lose

My mother was a letter-writer.

She wrote me a letter at the time of my birth. She wrote me a letter on every birthday. She wrote me letters at many other times when she was feeling deeply. Many of these I never saw until I went through her things after her death.

Here is one written on my fourteenth birthday. I received another letter on that day. This is the one I did not receive. It was not written to me. Instead it was written *about* me to God.

Midnight—and in the darkness not a stirring, not a sound, except the hushed breathing of a girl just turned fourteen. And I, her mother, sit by her bed watching while the moonbeams caress her cheeks. I send my petitions to Thee, my God, asking for Thy help so that I may be worthy of my motherood.

The room given to her has changed since the first time I sat beside her to write. The pink ruffles have given way to soft pleated drapes; the tiny table and chairs are in the attic and a cherished hope chest stands in the corner. The red-checked pinafores and high-top shoes are now obsolete in favor of plaid skirts, bright-colored sweaters, and high heels.

My daughter is no longer a child. She is becoming a woman. Her childhood is gone with the pink ruffles, the table and chairs, the red-checked pinafores. Adolescence is here with pleated drapes, a hope chest, and plaid skirts.

Maturity is just around the corner, and then she will be gone from my care. She will be gone from my home. I hold these hours as precious, for the days of my training will go too rapidly. Soon she will fashion a new life of her own.

As I stand above her this night, my God, I pray for wisdom in helping her to make this transition between childhood and maturity. Give me the ability to understand when she comes to me a young woman, and the ability to understand when the next moment she returns to me a little child.

This is a difficult age for her, Lord. She cannot return to childhood, nor has she attained maturity. May I, her mother, be enabled to give her the guidance to make the transition successfully so that she may reach the realm of fulfillment.

I ask Thee, Lord, to give me patience for her numerous parties filled with songs, giggles, and whispers. Help me to like her friends and welcome them to our home. Give me the ability to laugh with her, play with her, tease with her. Give me the sensitivity to comprehend her dreams. May she know every moment my love for her, my aspirations for her, my desires for her happiness.

During this period of adolescence, of transition, may I be enabled to give her courage to face the storms of life with head held high and heart unafraid. May I be enabled to give her strength to cope with the future ably and well. With eyes clear and bright, trust strong and deep, may she gain a true sense of values from me, her mother. O God, may I endow her life with gifts of far greater value than mere monetary possessions.

Through these teen years, Lord, help me to give

my child glowing memories filled with joy; a home rich with sympathy, tenderness, love, and truth. May I be able to hold her steady with discipline firm and strong—but softened by the kindness of my smile and the depth of understanding and compassion of my heart. Help me to give my little girl a glimpse of the glory of heaven. Through the example of my life, may I give her a sturdy faith.

Before this life was given to me, I wondered if I could love her with the deep, strong passion I had observed in other mothers of little girls. But when I saw her that first time, love enfolded me in such dazzling, fierce measure that I lifted my voice in gratitude and adoration for this, Thy heavenly gift to me. During the ensuing years of rattles, bottles, and teething rings—skates, dolls, and jump ropes—that love has grown each day.

But now, Lord, I earnestly pray for yet another gift. I ask for wisdom, guidance, and direction so that I may teach her, lead her, and guide her until she will find the fulfillment of Thy plan for her life on the plateau of maturity—so that one day she and I may safely enter Thy heavenly portals.

For my teen-ager, I ask that Thou wilt give her a mother who will be worthy of the wondrous cloak of motherhood.

Adolescence is the beginning step on a way apart from parents. Adolescence is the first brick in a world separate from home. The foundation is laid during childhood. Adolescence is the entryway to individuality. How wise the mother who understands A TIME TO LOSE!

A Time to Get

Some of my earliest recollections revolve around our time of family prayer. Twice every day of my life at

home, no matter how busy or how full, the family gathered about while Daddy read the Bible, and we knelt together and prayed.

I can remember sitting on the floor, cuddling my Pekinese dog, as the wind howled fiercely outside. But I was safe and warm inside where I sat before the bright flickering fire, while my mother sat calmly in the big armchair, and my father read from the great Book.

My father's face showed gentleness as some men's faces show vice and greed. His voice was rich and deep and broad, like a river stretching out into the ocean. When he read the chapter about love in the New Testament, the house resounded with music. It wasn't just the quality of his voice and the enunciation of the words; it was the spirit in him that caught up the words and seemed to kindle them like a flame.

My mother's face was soft with love. Her eyes communicated that she had looked upon all the tragedy and injustices of life and had determined to smile in spite of them. The tilt of her head, as she listened to the Bible reading, reflected the intensity of her interest, the openness of her trust.

Always a questioner, I would study her face in these moments. Did she really *believe* these words as divine truth? Were they truly the motivation of her life?

The room in which we held family prayer was shabby by modern standards, and Mother wore inexpensive, often ill-fitting clothes. Yet I knew her intense love of beauty. Was she merely a victim of circumstances, I often thought, or was she really joyfully giving up material beauty for the inner beauty of serving her God in the way she felt called?

The problems brought to our parsonage home were the cross section of all human woes. Mother worked with the young mother faced with the injustice of a baby born without arms. She knew of the inequities of life to people born of a different color; the heartaches of a wife with an alcoholic husband; the tragedy of a twelve-year-old bearing a baby following incestuous rape by her uncle.

The problems she personally faced were myriad. She knew the sting of sending her child to school in faded clothes because of poverty; the pain of unjust criticism which is the occupational hazard of living in a parsonage; the sorrow of having her love returned by hate and her gifts taken with ingratitude; the devastation of seeing her dearly loved son face illness in a place beyond her reach; the life-shattering pronouncement of an incurable illness breeding within her own body.

As I sat during family prayer time, I observed her serenity and peace, and I wondered. Could it be that religion *was* more than creed and doctrine? Could it be that religion *was* triumph?

As I entered adolescence and began seeking answers *I* could accept as truth, possibly the most influential moments were when my parents would get me still during family prayers. There was a splendid simplicity, an unshakeable honesty, an awesome power of the divine that instilled within me concepts from which I could never get away. Their faith at family prayer time was like a campfire on a dark night. It illuminated and warmed, and I never forgot.

How wise the mother who understands that home is not a place, but a *feeling*—something intangible and very precious! Home is the place where God dwells in the midst of humanity, when parents take TIME TO GET children quiet in the presence of their faith in, and communion with, the Almighty. This provides the foundation when, in maturity, children find the TIME TO GET a personal trust.

A Time to Kill

I was fourteen.

With all the fervor of a fourteen-year-old, I wanted to be in love. My inner joy, like a coiled spring, released itself in small irresistible smiles on all the world that first time he asked me to go steady.

My parents said, "No!" They said I could not date steadily at age fourteen. They watched as the laughter died in my eyes. They agonized as hatred for them filled me.

"You aren't fair," I lashed out. "You don't understand. Surely you don't understand. You are *destroying* my dreams!"

"Yes," my father sighed heavily. "We understand. But we feel there is a time in life when, to protect those we love, we have to kill dreams."

I raged. I fought.

I beat against the walls of their decision until my hands were bruised and broken. But their decision was firm.

I argued in earnest, bitter, strong, angry words, calculated to wound. But they remained immovable.

Days went by . . .

One evening my father came home early from the office. Mother was mending clothes in the living room where I had pulled the sewing machine to work on a dress.

My father began to talk to me about his reasons

for not wanting me to establish a steady dating relationship at such a young age. He talked about a mistake he had made in his life. He explained his desire to shield me from opportunities for mistakes until I was more mature. I understood his motivation.

A juncture.

The angry words were over. But their chill lay like a glacier across the room, silent and solid. There was a long, stinging pause to see whose hand would bridge the chasm, whose voice would bid the other come.

By all rights, it should have been mine.

I had been the one hating and lashing out. Any jury would have borne my parents out. But there was no jury, just the family with the silence hardening among us.

In that first moment, when choice was still possible, my father attempted to cross the glacier.

"Little girl," he said huskily, "we love you." And then he cried.

My heart, which had been stone-cold with hatred, melted and tears scalded my cheeks.

Then I was in their arms, and we were together again—the three of us. Although I did not say it, I admitted to myself that I was not wise enough to guide my life, and that although I pushed against their boundaries, I felt secure within them. I needed the strength of my mother and father when I was weak and uncertain myself.

This need is universal with all children.

Parents who care deeply enough will take strong, invincible stands at certain points of life, even though those moments bring tears and bitterness. Wise are the parents who know there is indeed A TIME TO KILL.

A Time to Refrain From Embracing

I decided to enter a ceramics contest.

Mother helped me with the molds and offered suggestions about color tones. I worked for weeks.

Jane was my friend. She decided to enter the same contest the night before the judging. Hastily she went to work, and with the mold still a bit damp, she placed it in competition.

Jane won second place.

I didn't win anything.

Rushing home, I expected Mother to enfold me with her loving sympathy. But when she heard the results, she said sternly, "Don't plan to go to your room to cry. You need to face up to something about life. Bitter as it may be, there are some things each person cannot do perfectly, while another person can achieve perfection with a fourth of the time and effort. You are not especially talented in working with ceramics. You must learn for yourself what your limitations are and accept yourself with those limitations."

"I can't do *anything*," I began to wail.

"I told you not to cry," she said firmly. "You have discovered something about yourself today. Now with that knowledge, simply turn your energies from the areas where you are limited to the areas where you can excel."

"We-l-l-l, I *can* write poetry and Jane can't."

"If you're good in poetry, then become very good. This is what you should learn from the defeat of today: self-knowledge of limitations and determination to develop the skills you do have."

So I didn't cry over the ceramics contest although I had fully expected to. Instead I grabbed my tablet and went for a walk in the woods. I wrote some poetry. And that spring, I won a state contest.

Mother had demanded I accept my limitations and channel my energies—not in self-pity or hopeless struggling—but into something in which I could excel.

I took violin lessons throughout grade school so I could eventually play in the high school orchestra. My father moved to a new church just as I was ready to enter high school. There was no orchestra.

Totally disappointed, I moped for days. Finally, Mother said, "Let's talk."

I knew my moping was going to end one way or another. When she said "Let's talk" in that tone of voice, I knew I might as well give up.

Grudgingly, I sat down.

"All right. You wanted to be in the orchestra. Now it is impossible. Let's try to discover what you wanted to get out of the orchestra."

"Well, it would be fun to work with a group. I could develop excellence as a performer. It would be an avenue of achievement and I could fulfill my love of competition in contests."

She listened carefully.

'Is there another way you could attain these same things?"

"How should I know?"

"By considering carefully."

I rolled my eyes.

She ignored my dramatics.

"How about speech? Plays and debates call for a group effort. You could develop excellence as a performer. In these areas and in public speaking, you could compete and achieve."

Well!

That was a new thought!

I loved speech. Could it be?

Yes, it could. Although denied one avenue of accomplishment, I found another, which for me, with my particular abilities, proved to be much better in the long run.

My experience in drama, debate, and extemporaneous speech eventually led me to a scholarship and ultimately to a position as professor in the field. In retrospect, I can believe it was better for *me* to be in a school without an orchestra, for God had something in mind that would be more fulfilling for *me*.

Mother tried to teach me that God allows failure and frustration to enter our lives, for through these experiences, we learn to trust Him more implicitly. The negative answers I received to my requests to win a ceramics contest and to play the violin in a high school orchestra were a part of His plan in shaping me into something bigger and finer than my dreams could imagine. Mother helped me to believe that defeat and frustration did not have to be dead-end streets.

A mother can change failure and frustration into stepping stones to success when she is wise enough to know the difference between a time to embrace and A TIME TO REFRAIN FROM EMBRACING.

A Time to Break Down

When I was fifteen, my mother became ill. It was the beginning stages of what was later diagnosed as Parkinson's disease. Stiffness took control of her body almost overnight. She could not move at all without assistance.

She had to make the adjustment from happy, healthy wife and mother to invalid. And if the adjustment was difficult (as I now know it had to be), she never allowed me to feel it.

Her zest for living remained keen; her love for God remained constant; her faith became even more triumphant.

One day as I was dusting, I found my father's wallet, which he had left on the dresser. Curiously, I opened it and found only a couple of dollars. I knew medical expenses were high because of my mother's illness. Even at age fifteen, I was aware of financial problems.

Concerned, I took the wallet to Mother and asked, "Is this all the money we have?"

She smiled her usual happy smile. I could find no trace of worry as she replied, "Yes, Honey. But our heavenly Father is rich."

She must have seen the doubt within me because she picked up the Bible that was always at her side and read, "Seek ye first the kingdom of God, and his righteousness; and all these things shall be added unto you."

She took my hand. "We are fulfilling the first part of this promise to the best of our ability. Would it not be sinful to doubt that God would fulfill His part?"

"Sinful!" I was shocked at the strong word she associated with disbelief.

"When we worry about money problems, it is a sure sign we do not believe in God's ownership of earth's resources."

Always the skeptic, I looked at my father's almost empty wallet. Involuntarily, I shook my head.

"If you concentrate on those few bills," she cautioned, "you will develop a 'poverty complex' and that is dangerous business. By doing so, you deny the fact that you are a child of the King. By doing so, you insult His Word."

My eyes spilled tears.

"Mother, I want to believe," I whispered.

"Although we don't have a large quantity of this world's goods, we have more than enough. We have a warm home, clothing, food, love. All of the children have gone to college, just as you will go when the time comes.

"When we seek first the kingdom of God and His righteousness, we have no right to worry about material goods. Not if we believe the Bible as God's Word. He *promised* that 'all these things shall be added.' "

I sat down beside her.

"Honey, you haven't had time in your life to test God's Word. Now is a good time to begin. And I can testify to you from the vantage point of my years that God's Word will never fail. You don't have to be afraid. In more lavish abundance than is necessary, God will add 'all these things.' Trust Him and you'll see."

And I did.

With my ever-questioning nature, I watched carefully, observed closely. And I discovered that "all these things" were added in the right time and in the right way. Never a moment too soon. But never a moment too late.

It was a discovery from which I could never get away. That experience laid a cornerstone on which ultimately I built my own personal faith.

The problems of life are first encountered in the home-life of a child. Terror can corrode his being unless he has a mother who is perceptive enough to dispel fear in A TIME TO BREAK DOWN.

A Time to Laugh

The first summer Mother was ill, my father took
her to a mineral-bath resort. I suppose you would call it
a resort. They gave mineral baths, but there the
resemblance to the usual conception of a resort ended.
Because Father had to tend to his pastoral duties, he
deposited Mother and me in a small rock cabin on the
grounds of the bathhouse in this tiny village and left
Mother in my care.

Mother was so stiffened she could not move
without assistance. She was without teeth, because they
had been removed early in her illness, as a possible
source of infection. No new ones had been made for her
at that time. To complicate matters even further, when
she began taking the baths, her body reacted and
swelled to twice its normal size.

So there I was!

Little in my fifteen years had prepared me for this.

Mother had to have a special diet. This I prepared
on a two-burner hot plate. First I ground the food so she
could eat it without chewing, and then I fed her each bite.

Her bed linen had to be washed daily. I took a
bucket to a well where I pumped water, carried it back
to the cabin, heated it, and then washed the clothes,
using a scrub board.

It was summertime and so we needed ice, which
we secured from the local iceman in fifty-pound blocks.
These I put in our icebox, and they melted into a pan

underneath. I always forgot the pan, so this provided delightful moments of mopping to add to the other new experiences.

I had to help Mother in and out of bed. Once she was in one position, she would remain there until I moved her. I slept on a cot by the side of her bed, and she called me during the night when she needed to change positions.

Only a few months before she had been in complete control of her life. Now she suffered all the indignities of having to be cared for like a baby.

Someone once asked me, "How did your mother react to illness?"

I thought about it for only a moment.

"Well, "I replied, "she laughed a lot."

My most vivid memory of that period was Mother's ability to see the ridiculous in the tragic. Whether she was attempting to swallow the insipid ground liver I served her or whether she was being clumsily placed on the bed by my inept efforts, she saw the humor.

Many times I would struggle to get her in a comfortable position on the bed. I would tug and pull and push. When I would finally suceed and straighten up to look at her, she would be full of laughter.

"Why on earth are you laughing?" I would demand angrily.

There was a mist in her eyes when she replied, "But Honey, it's better to laugh than to cry!"

When the icebox overran, she would call out, "Run for the ark; the flood is upon us."

When I burned her food, she sent me into fits of laughter by reciting in a grave encyclopedic fashion: "Carbon is excellent for the digestion. When food is cooked to a nice black crisp, its vitamin value is instantly increased."

Once in trying to turn her, I dropped her on the floor. Tears of terror and shame spilled down my cheeks as I tugged to get her back on the bed. When I succeeded, she was laughing again.

"Mother, are you all right?"

"Right as Goliath—and great was the fall thereof," she intoned.

That hot little cabin with all its inconveniences and pain held much more laughter than tears that summer.

Once I asked, "Mother, don't you mind this stiffness and pain?"

"I mind for you and your father and the other children because you have to worry about me. But I look out upon the world, and the fact that my body is filled with pain and stiffness hasn't changed the world a bit. It's as full of beauty and excitement as ever."

Laughter comes at comedy times, party times, game times, and whenever an individual has the courage to seek it. A mother who can lead a child to laughter in the midst of pain, alien surroundings, and frustration is indeed rare. This mother teaches her child that one can create, even in the midst of sorrow, A TIME TO LAUGH.

A Time for War

Marie was my friend. My father taught a Sunday school class in her part of town. I met her and loved her. She came to my house. I went to hers.

My school chum, Kathy, came with me to Marie's one day, and we worked up a trio. We had a "great sound." We worked it out with Mother that we would sing in church on Sunday. I could hardly wait.

By the time we were halfway through the first stanza, I felt it, though I didn't know what it was. But I felt it. And the prickles of resentment went all over my scalp as we finished the song. I knew we were a great trio, but there was surely something wrong.

When we were seated, my father praised the trio. Then I felt it even stronger. But I still didn't know what it was.

After church, Marie left immediately. I stood with Kathy trying to figure out what was wrong.

A lady walked by, looked at us coldly and said, "Don't dare ever desecrate our church like that again."

Then we knew what it was.

Marie was black.

I went home in tears of anger and frustration. Even though I was a child of the South, my parents had kept me from even considering prejudice. A human being was a human being. A child of God was a child of God. No differences.

Now, for the first time, I faced this injustice, and I burned.

When my father came home for lunch, I gave vent to all my anger. He listened quietly and said, "Why don't you call Marie and ask her to sing with you and Kathy tonight?"

I looked at him incredulously.

"In spite of?"

"In spite of!" he said flatly.

And we did.

No matter how carefully parsonage parents may try to shield a child from church battles, it is impossible. I heard it at school the next day.

A family in the church was threatening to drop its membership if I continued my friendship with Marie. They were going to demand that my father make me break any ties with the girl.

I was heartsick at causing my father such a tremendous problem. I knew he had enough concerns without my causing another.

I went home at lunch and told Mother I was going to call Marie and explain everything. She would understand, and we would just not see each other again.

Mother didn't say anything for a long time. When she finally spoke, her words were measured as if she were pronouncing something of great importance. "We are peace-loving people. But the Bible tells us there comes a time for war. I believe that time has arrived. You will not be a quitter."

My heart leaped.

There was steel inside this soft-spoken, loving lady. She would claim no rights for herself, but she would fight for the rights of others. I was proud.

The people left the church membership. I maintained my friendship with Marie. She and Kathy and I still had a "great sound." But I never forgot Mother's proclamation of war.

Social injustices and inequities confront all of us. Closing one's eyes, giving in to pressure, may be the easiest way of handling such problems. But it is not the best way. Strong are the children whose mother instills within them that, in everyone's life, there does come A TIME FOR WAR!

A Time to Speak

Are you getting serious about Roger?''

My brother had come home for a weekend and had observed the class ring and oversized jacket, both symbols of going steady.

I looked at him in astonishment.

Going steady was a high school phenomenon. But at this stage, it had no more to do with diamond rings than the books about Dick and Jane had to do with a university.

''Of course not! He is fun and I like him. I am certainly not 'getting serious!' ''

He looked relieved.

''Just wondered.''

''Well, don't!'' I told him. ''I may be an idealist who never gets married. But at least I will always be an idealist. He may not come in shining armor on a white stallion, but he will be quite princely before I 'get serious.' ''

Mother was working in the kitchen, but she had overheard the conversation. That night she came into my room and we talked.

''I was glad to hear your declaration of idealism. Don't ever let it go.''

I nodded, and we sat silent for a long time.

Mother had grown up in a Puritan family where marriage and sex were never discussed. She had determined that her girl-child would not grow up to be

so ignorant. From my first glimmerings of curiosity, she had given clear definitive answers.

Along with the biological facts, she always included an aura of reverence. "Your marriage may be the most beautiful, most awesome experience of your life," she often said. And from her attitude had evolved my idealism.

All of the small conversations that had come through the years with the ebb and flow of my curiosity reached their climax that evening.

After a long period of silence, Mother said: "I have talked to you many times, many ways. But tonight let me try to put it down specifically so you will clearly know my philosophy, which I hope you will adopt for yourself.

"The price tag on real love is high, but it is always worth the self-discipline involved. The down payment for the shoddy imitation is low, but you pay installments for the rest of your life. You save sex for marriage even when heart and mind are persuasive, even when it seems so right your whole body aches.

"You are a woman—not just a female or a girl-child—and as a woman, you are partner of man. This partnership can create a beautiful new world in which you and the children you produce may grow and live. This is your basic career. The only way to guarantee that some man will cherish you as his partner in this creation is to be worthy of love."

The breeze ruffled the curtains. We sat together pondering.

"And even when your 'prince' comes, you wait until the right time, the right place. Only then can your marriage have the excitement, the lasting joy. Do it any other way and you lose something—forever."

I nodded soberly and made solemn promises within myself.

On issues of importance, a mother may be the strongest molding influence in a child's life. But the timing must be right. Ever observant, perceiving, feeling, a mother will catch the exact moment in her child's life when it is A TIME TO SPEAK.

A Time to Keep Silence

The letter was written on yellow stationery. I knew its sender immediately. Dena always wrote on yellow stationery.

Eagerly I tore it open to read its contents. A few minutes later, the pages fell limply from my hands.

"I won't meet you at college next week as planned. I've decided to go to New York instead. I've met this great guy, and we are going to share an apartment in the city.

"I think it sounds wild. Marriage is dull and safe. I'm going to have a ball!"

I could hardly believe the message scrawled on the yellow stationery.

"You'll go on to college, of course, but think of all the fun you'll miss. The social code is changing. Why don't you wise up, too?"

I handed the letter to Mother silently.

She read it and stood studying me carefully. I knew she wanted to say something. I could feel the defenses, the philosophies, the rebuttals churning within her.

But it wasn't the time and she sensed it. Regretfully, I think.

We looked at each other. My eyes were direct, but guarded. I did not want philosophy now.

Then she smiled—wistfully.

"I've already rested my case a long time ago," she said, as she walked out of the room.

Five days from college, I was facing life on my own. I could look at life, the changing social code, great guys—just as Dena had—and I had to make choices. My own choices.

Many mothers alienate themselves when they cannot learn to respect the growing maturity of their children. In the formative years, teaching is imperative. But just as there is a time to speak, so the wise mother perceives A TIME TO KEEP SILENCE.

A Time to Sew

The day I left for college, my parents returned home in silence. My mother told me later that as soon as they arrived, my father went directly to his office in the church next door to the parsonage. She went into the house and walked through its emptiness to my room. She stood poised in the door—remembering my joys, my tears, my carelessness, and my growing carefulness. Then she knelt beside my bed.

Probably in those moments of agony, she faced up to the imperative of her release of my life. A new era had dawned. Her last child had left home. She and my father now faced the rest of their lives without us children.

Never a person to give in to self-pity or moping over the difficulty of facing passing worlds, she soon rose to her feet, went to my father's office, and invited him for a trip in the country.

That first day, they were not in an empty house luxuriating in the pain of their tears. They were picnicking in a nearby canyon and visiting friends in a nearby city. Indomitable, my mother was determined to build another world—one which would contain adventure and delight and challenge—just as the world of children had.

Always active in the church, she redoubled her efforts. She set aside a special day of each week to bake rolls and cobblers for the ill, or those who lived alone.

On still another day, she delivered her goodies.

She had always wanted to work with ceramics, and so she enrolled in a course. There was also a course in flower-arranging, which had always been one of her special loves. What fun!

Her letters to me were not sighs for my homecoming, but recounts of her new adventures and activities. Although she was deeply interested in my life, I knew she was not dependent upon it. She had an exciting world all her own.

After my marriage, she began a new project. Although I had grown up in a parsonage, I discovered as a minister's wife that I needed additional information and help. Mother began to delve into all her collected writings and projects so she could send me program ideas, tips for parties, ways of handling a missionary society, *ad infinitum*.

When I faced my first vacation Bible school as a minister's wife, Mother, age sixty-three, came to help. My father held a revival for us in the evening, and my mother worked with me on the difficult job of supervising a thriving Bible school during the day.

Motherhood is a changing phenomenon. It is an all-consuming world of sewing for children for many years. Then it demands a metamorphosis. The dependent become independent. The sewing hand is idle unless the mother is versatile, flexible, and indomitable enough to turn her attention to sewing for herself—and other people—in a new world.

Challenging times for a mother: a time to sew for her children, a time to let them go, a time to find a new field and begin again. Wise is the mother who finds that when her children are all gone away, it is still A TIME TO SEW.

A Time to Hate

"Hate error; seek truth."

This was the postscript Mother scribbled on the first letter she wrote to me after my arrival at college. It was almost prophetic. Maybe it truly was.

Perhaps she knew her child well enough to sense the storm of doubt into which I would be cast that first semester away from home. Perhaps she felt it. I am not sure. But it proved to be true.

Suddenly on my own, without the guiding hand of my parents, I realized my philosophy of life could no longer be secondhand. I had to *choose* for myself the things I would accept as truth.

I began reading a book on the psychology of religion. The seething, agonizing doubts about all the fundamentals of life hurled themselves at me at top speed. But I kept reading the book; I kept searching for truth.

Perhaps I may subconsciously have been wise enough to understand that if my religion was to remain the vital and honest force in my life it had always been, I must never run from the search for truth.

I continued to read.

The darkness grew heavier.

I remember one night standing by my dormitory window looking out at the rain pouring from blackened skies. I said aloud to myself, "I have never felt so lonely in my life."

It was then I decided to call Mother. Collect.

By the time she had accepted the charges, I had burst into tears. Just the sound of her voice was reassuring.

"Mother," I wept, "I don't know why I'm crying. I don't know what is wrong. You know that book I told you about. Oh, I'm so mixed up! I don't know what I believe."

And when I had spilled it all out, she said quietly, "Honey, you are in college. Your mind is expanding. It is quite normal, even essential, for you to consider seriously the meaning of life and God. When you find these questions rising within you, don't run away. Face the doubts and problems honestly and courageously until you find the answers."

"How will I know if I find the *right* answers?"

"You will know because God will guide you."

Her voice communicated her suffering with me as she said, "No matter where your thinking may have led you, you will know you still have God. You have only to reach upward for Him. The Lord is your shepherd."

I hung up the phone. But there was no peace. I had to discover truth on my own.

The next morning during breakfast, I left the meal early and went to sit in the parlor. An older girl, whom I did not know, came and sat across from me. She pointed to the book in her hands, "It's Whittier," she said, and commenced reading.

I sat in my maze of intellectual gymnastics. If this was truth—but how could I *know* if it was truth? And if not, then. . .

My mind whirled on and on in an endless tunnel of darkness.

Suddenly the girl leaned toward me.

"I must read you this," she said. "It's so beautiful that I cannot keep it to myself:

> So in the maddening maze of things
> And tossed by storm and flood,
> To one fixed trust my spirit clings;
> I know that God is good.

Isn't it magnificent?"

I nodded my agreement while my mind fastened itself to the phrase, "maddening maze of things." This Whittier had surely described my emotional state.

"To one fixed trust my spirit clings." But I had no "fixed trust" any more. How could I ever *know*?

The bells chimed then, and I rushed off to class.

This was a church college, and every class period was opened with prayer. I paid little attention as the professor began to pray in his customary way. But somewhere in that prayer my head came up, and my eyes keenly searched the professor's face.

I do not remember exactly what he said, but in essence he was stating, "I am grateful that we do not have to strain to understand Your person or Your ways. Intellectually, we do not have to understand theology. We have only to relax, expose our hearts to Your love,

and know that, all unannounced, all unsought, You will come to us."

In that moment, I knew this was the truth I would accept for myself. I would believe God was. Although I could not explain all the points of theology, I would *choose* to believe God existed.

"The Lord is my shepherd," I whispered and the music of those words released the tightness of despair within me. My eyes felt the hot sting of tears. In a great wave, peace came to me for the first time in days, and I was at rest.

"The Lord is my shepherd," I wrote the fine old words over and over on my notebook. I knew this was the cornerstone on which I would build my personal faith.

"Hate error," Mother had said. "Seek truth." She had not been afraid for the questions to come. For only through honest doubt can sincere faith become a reality. One cannot find personal answers until he has asked questions.

She had instilled within me a hatred for the false. I could not accept anything as basic to my life simply because someone else said it was true. I had to seek truth for myself.

And I found it capsulized in one phrase of ancient Scripture, "The Lord is my shepherd." I could not prove it mathematically, scientifically, or logically. I would not try. I would simply relax, expose myself to His love, and *believe* in the personality of God. This was my *choice*.

Developing adults stand at a crossroads where no one can stand with them. The choice of a life faith, an enveloping life philosophy has to be made alone. A mother, if she would be most helpful to her child, understands this need to displace error with truth—this time when, if fallacy can be found, it is A TIME TO HATE.

A Time to Pluck Up That Which Is Planted

When I went away to college, it was a painful time for Mother. I was her only girl-baby, her last child.

At some point in my first year, she wrote this letter. I did not find it until after she had lost consciousness in her last illness. But it was written to me in my eighteenth year.

I do not know why I never received it. Perhaps it was too much of a mother's heart. Perhaps I was not wise enough then to understand.

My dearest young woman,

Clocks steadily tick-tock and tell each hour in its turn. They do not jump eighteen years without notice. Or at least they are not supposed to. And yet it seems so short a time ago you lay against my heart a baby thing.

But now I look over and see you there—the soft light shining on your brown hair—and I know you are no longer a child. You stand on the threshold of life, and all the prizes hang like bags of candy on a Christmas tree, and you can take your choice.

But choices are eternal, little girl.

Choices shape your life.

Choices determine your destiny.

In these next few years, you will *choose* what kind of woman you will be. You will *choose* whether you will meet life with a frown or a smile, whether you will be minutely self-righteous or strong enough to say "I'm sorry," whether you will live to please yourself or to help others.

As you face womanhood, you will *choose* whether you will meet people with harsh criticism and unbending standards or whether you will meet people with your heart whispering:

> If I could only see the road you came
>   The jagged rocks and crooked ways,
> I would more kindly think of your missteps
>   And only praise.

> If I could know the heartaches you have felt,
>   The longings for the things that never came,
> I would not misconstrue your erring then
>   Nor even blame.

As you face womanhood, you will *choose* the way you will meet the storm, for there will be times when all your world will be violent upheaval. Will you be overcome, or will you stand serene and strong? The choice will be yours. The secret is on whom will you focus: yourself or others?

But, you may ask, what if others have caused the storm? What then?

The choice is yours, young woman. Will you *choose* to be bitter and resentful, or will you *choose* to be forgiving and forgetful?

"But how can I forget the unkind things that are said, the cruel and unfair treatment that I have received?" you ask.

I only know of one sure way. Search yourself in the light of the incident, and see how you may profit by the pain. Then *choose* to forget it. Never talk about it, and never think about it. Never speak even to your best friend about it. When it bobs into your mind,

banish it at once. It will surprise you how quickly you can forget when you *choose* to forget.

As you face womanhood, you will *choose* the way you will meet joy and triumph, for there will be times when life will be a glorious circle. In those moments, will you be grateful or arrogant? Will you be awed or proud? Will you be giving or receiving? The choice is yours.

As you stand on the threshold of life, and all the prizes hang like bags of candy on a Christmas tree, you must take your choice.

You must *choose* the level of education you will achieve.

You must *choose* the profession you will pursue.

You must *choose* the degree of excellence you will atain.

You must *choose* the man with whom you want to spend the rest of your life.

You must *choose* the kind of woman you will be.

Dear young woman, as you stand on the threshold of life, and all the prizes hang like bags of candy on a Christmas tree, you can take your choice. But remember *choices are eternal.*

I sit here and look at your flowing brown hair, your youthful form, and my heart aches to hold you steady, insist you use my maturity. I want intensely to push you aside, step into your place, and make the choices for you.

> My love wants only the highest and the best
> for you, my child—but my love is not enough!
> I know that the world's wintry storms
>   will attack so hard,
>   they will blow out
>   the candle of your trust,
>   your faith,
>   that would guide your choices
>   in life.
> But I can give you no certain armor
>   against the storm
>   unless I learn release.
>
> My love is not enough.
>
> But God, too, wants only the
> highest and the best for you.
> My child, place your hand in His.
> Here is your armor against the storm.
> He will guide you to life's finest joys.
> My love is not enough.
> I must release you.
> The choices must be yours in A TIME TO
> PLUCK UP THAT WHICH IS PLANTED.

A Time to Rend

The time for their traditional retirement came and went. They did not notice.

But ultimately my mother's health deteriorated to the point where they knew a change had to be made. So my father bought a house in their hometown, and they retired. Although Mother could still walk when that decision was made, soon after the move she was forced into a wheelchair.

That was when I began to worry about her in earnest. But I had no need to.

Although in a wheelchair, Mother was as robust as a dandelion, going on year after year as strong as ever—sometimes stronger. She had a special day when she would go to the home of a blind friend and read to her, and they would memorize Scripture together. She began scrapbooks for her grandson. She continued working with her ceramics and flowers, keeping the homes of those she knew decorated.

She continued to give piano lessons. She still worked with her lifetime collection of parsonage material so I could have it for use in my parsonage. She wrote long letters to her children and friends. People who barely knew her have reported receiving letters and notes of cheer sent out of her overflowing heart of love for all and written by ever-stiffening but ever-busy hands.

She wrapped her life in her children so long as we

were hers to mold. But when the time came, she released us to ourselves and took on the task of sewing for herself and other people in a new world.

On a college campus I met a young man who was the epitome of all my dreams. When he asked me for a date, I danced with joy in my room (after a nonchalant, casual acceptance to him, of course). When he asked me to marry him, I looked forward to a life of fulfillment.

On the eve of my wedding, my mother wrote me her thoughts. I found the letter tucked under my pillow when I awoke on my wedding day.

My Dear Daughter:

You were so small so short a time ago
   You lay against my heart a baby thing,
And now I watch the lovely flush and glow
   Illumine you that only love can bring.

They told me I should feel hot, jealous pain
   When first you turned to other arms from mine;
I have not found it so. Not loss, but gain
   It is for me, you've found a thing so fine.

I love him with a strange and tender love—
   This fine sweet boy, whose laughing,
      clear young eyes
Saw dreams come true in you, and sought to prove
   You not a child, but woman, woman wise.

You love absorbed. I see you wholly his,
   As he is yours until the end of time.
And yet—for tonight I know you are still
   In some way wholly, deeply, sweetly mine.

It is tradition with us that we exchange letters of love on our important days. Other than the day you made a decision for Christ, this is your most

important day. And I have thought long about what I could say to you that would be helpful to you in the new world you will be entering tomorrow.

For when you walk down the aisle in your lovely satin dress, you will be leaving the world we have created for you, and you will be launching upon the task of building a new one for yourself and for Bill.

I find that I want, most of all, to give you a formula for a successful marriage, which is our greatest desire for you. I think I have it. It is, in two short words, *pray together*. That sounds like a simple formula, doesn't it?

But don't let its simplicity deceive you. It takes work and discipline and *caring* to learn to pray together effectively. But it will be in the school of prayer that you will be able to resolve your differences.

I know, Honey, for it has been on our knees together in God's presence that your father and I have surmounted our differences and molded our lives into a oneness.

In our years in the pastorate, I have observed closely dozens, even hundreds, of brides and grooms who went forth to create a new world. Those who came back to us with a broken marriage had created a hellish world. But not one of those who failed prayed together. They intended to. In premarital counselling, they promised to. But in the hard everyday world, they found it easier to fight than to pray, easier to slam the door behind them than to kneel humbly in His presence asking for help.

I read some statistics that said the ratio of broken homes of families who pray together is one in five hundred. That is a pretty impressive figure when compared to the one in three broken marriages, which is now the general statistic.

You believe that God is love. You believe it was He who prepared you for each other. You believe His blessing will crown your marriage. Isn't it logical to believe, then, that the key to a successful marriage is to keep His love flowing into your love—expanding, overcoming, pushing out the boundaries, pushing over the hard places?

The more His love flows into your love, the happier and more radiant your marriage will be. I have tried it—and now I offer it to you—these two successful small words as your basic formula for a successful marriage. I promise.

Tomorrow evening, I will whisper goodbye to the little girl in the pink-ruffled pinafore, to the little girl with the blue bicycle and the fuzzy brown dog, to the little girl with the broken dolls and skinned knees.

In the candlelit church when the organ plays Mendelssohn, I will whisper goodbye to you in my heart. For I know you will never be just *my* little girl again. You will be Bill's wife. He will come first. That is the way it is supposed to be, and I would not want to change it. But tonight, this last night you will be home with us, I want to give you this letter as a token of my love. I pray, dear little girl, that your marriage will center always in the holy moments of prayer where two lives are united in sacred unity.

To every mother-child relationship there comes a time of transition. Some mothers cripple their children by tightly holding on to strings of love. Others freely release them to build new worlds for themselves, and in so doing, find their children returning to them as friends. How wise the mother who gladly bears the pain and wisely accepts A TIME TO REND.

A Time of Peace

Mother was in the hospital.

We drove all night to get to her.

Every turn of the tires seemed to echo the cry of my heart, "Don't die, Mother. I'm coming. I'm coming."

She barely knew consciously that I was there. I wanted to think she knew unconsciously, for her hand would still wrap itself tightly about mine in the same old way.

When we met with the doctor, he assured us she could never return home. She would require special care. He suggested a rest home.

I looked at my father. Fiercely independent, he had cared for Mother's needs alone. He had cooked her meals, washed her clothes, and combed her hair. He did not want to let her go to a rest home.

But in the end, he agreed. And after a few trial weeks that proved their unhappiness in separation, he went to live with her in the rest home.

Mother responded to the treatment and was "herself" again. My father wanted to take her home.

But Mother knew her illness had now taken its last tenacious hold. She had fought it valiantly through the years, but it was winning. Although remaining in the home meant leaving a dearly loved familiar world and entering a strange new one, my mother was game.

She made friends with all of the nurses and loved them like her own children. She made friends with the other people in the home and shared pictures of children and grandchildren.

She never realized she was a senior citizen in a rest home. She was Mrs. Wood living across the hall from Mrs. Lambert, Mrs. Rogers, Mrs. Donalds, and Mr. Snyder. They were all friends who shared together.

Although she was in a wheelchair, she attended the singing each Tuesday night in the parlor, the Sunday services held by the Christian church, and visited her friends. And she continued her zest for life.

She read books, played records, painted small ceramics, worked on scrapbooks for her grandsons, wrote letters, inspected flowers growing in the window, and loved everyone about her.

Then blindness overtook her.

She still tried to write to me at least once a week. She wrote in very large letters, and they ambled up and down the page, often into each other—but I could make them out.

Soon even this was denied her.

In her world of darkness, she listened to the television, had my father help her memorize Scripture, and enjoyed spelling games and Bible quizzes with everyone who would play with her.

When alone, she would try spelling words backwards and quoting poetry backwards—just for fun. And she smiled! To everyone who entered the room she gave a smile and her love.

Her indomitable cheerfulness and optimism were amazing. I told my brother one time that if we were to leave Mother in a deserted building in the middle of a desert without food and water, she would spend the remainder of her life smiling and rejoicing in our love because she would *know* we did it for her own good. She never doubted for a moment that the world was filled with beauty and joy.

My father read the Bible to her several hours every day. She spent a great deal of time in prayer, and the dominant note was thanksgiving. Often I stood by her bed and listened to her gratitude for the fulfillment of a lifetime, for each small joy that came to her during the last days of darkness and pain.

My heart would bow before such majesty. We are human beings, but we can, with God's help, make ourselves into royalty. I know. My mother did.

One of the last times I talked to Mother before she entered her final unconsciousness, I asked how she managed to be so radiant in a rest home. She did not hestitate for an answer.

"Honey, I passed my allotted threescore years and ten before I came here. These are bonus years, and because we are here they are good years. Here in this home, I have found a spontaneous lovingkindness that gives me a blessed sense of security.

"I can think of my sons, happy and successful in their various fields of work. I can think of my little girl writing professionally, teaching in college, fulfilling so many of my own dreams. And I can think of my husband who has proven his love a million times every day during these painful years. Tell me, *how* could I possibly be unhappy?"

Realistic as always, I said, "But Mother, you are bound to wish for your own home, your sight, and your health."

She nodded.

"Of course, there is some pain on those points, but when it is cushioned by gratitude, I find life to be *very good!*"

Life brings a riot of activity, demands, interests, and accomplishments, and when a mother is wise enough to focus on gratitude, in the end it will bring A TIME OF PEACE.

A Time to Die

Mother was unconscious for thirteen months before her death. Many times I raced the three hundred miles to the rest home, expecting to meet the crisis. But her strong heart kept beating.

Early one Saturday morning, the phone rang. This time I knew there was no hope. I was afraid I would not be able to get there in time. Somehow I felt I could not bear not to be there.

When I arrived, the feeding tubes had been removed. She was receiving no nourishment to sustain her; her body had rejected it all. But her heartbeat was strong.

My brothers came, and with our father we stood by her for six days. Amazingly, her heart kept beating in spite of lack of food or water. When it ceased, I was standing alone by her bed.

"Mother," my heart pleaded, "can't you say something? Please don't leave without saying *something*."

And as she drew her last breath, I felt a sense of peace. She didn't need to say anything now. She had dialogued with me all of my life. It had all been said. Her legacy was mine. It needed no postscripts.

I ran down the hall to where my brothers were sleeping in another room. They came immediately. My husband encircled my waist with his arms as my brother, Joe, went to Daddy, who lay asleep in his bed alongside Mother's.

Daddy awakened to Joe's gentle touch.

"What happened?" he asked quickly.

"Mother went to heaven a few minutes ago," Joe said.

My heart constricted.

This was the moment I had dreaded.

My father had loved Mother in a rare and beautiful way. The last years he had waited on her every need with wholehearted devotion. For the last thirteen months, he had watched over her like a mother hen with one chick.

I was so afraid he would go to pieces in this moment. But I was not reckoning with the Gibraltar faith and strength of my father. He didn't say anything for a moment. Then he smiled a wistful smile as the tears welled in his eyes. "She's happy."

"Oh Daddy, yes she is," said Joe. "If Jesus told us the truth, she is able to see for the first time in months; she is able to run for the first time in years; she is able to sing with the most joyous abandon."

I stood by my mother's still, lifeless body, and my heart whispered, "Oh God, thank You that I *know* it is not my mother who has died. It is only her shell. She has a new body now *with You*. And no one could ever enjoy it more!"

Daddy said quietly, "I don't know how her heart kept beating for so long."

"We always knew her heart was the most remarkable thing about her," Joe said, smiling through his tears. "Both physically and spiritually."

Oh yes, I thought, *we shall always remember her as a Great Heart!*

The men came from the funeral home. We remained with the body as they prepared it for transferral. I watched as they lifted the stiff legs, which had so long refused to respond to her commands. I saw the flesh on the bedsores tear as they rolled the body, and I *knew* that, although I loved the body she had occupied, it was not she. She had been released.

One of the last letters Mother ever wrote to me in her large scrawling letters spelled out how she wanted me to feel at the time of her death. Here is the letter:

I have been thinking of how close we have been through the years of your life. You came to me, a gift from the hand of God, and I have rejoiced in that gift ever since. We have experienced joy and sorrow, tragedy and triumph together.

But now as I approach the time of my going home, I want to tell you something that you must remember when you are bidding my body goodbye. My child, do not ever say, "Mother is dead." Just know that I'm away; I've gone on ahead to a better land, and one day you will come and we shall again join hands.

Don't think of my sadness at leaving this world where I have known so much joy. Instead, little girl, think of your mother stepping on a shore and finding it heaven; of her taking hold of a hand and finding it God's hand; of her breathing a new air and finding it celestial air; of her feeling invigorated and finding it immortality; of her stepping from storm and darkness and tempest to an unknown calm. Think of your mother waking up and finding it Home."

When we returned from the rest home that early Friday morning, I took this letter from my suitcase and read it to my husband. He took me in his arms, and I cried. Tears of rejoicing for her; tears of suffering for me.

My brothers and I planned her funeral service. My cousin made her a beautiful pink dress. We selected a bronze casket with soft pink lining. Pink was her color.

Flowers and friends began arriving.
I stood by her casket.
This poem, written on the day of the funeral,
expresses the feelings this daughter felt as her mother's
body lay in state:

February 22, 1971

My mother's body lies in a pink-lined casket.
Her familiar hands are folded;
    her always-smiling face is serene.
People come and say goodbye as if they believe
    she is dead.
By their tears of finality I can see
    they have missed the whole point of death.

My mother was full of
    bright life,
    easy laughter,
    quick forgiveness,
    indomitable bravery,
    quicksilver delight.
And when her body wore out, she went away.
Don't you see?
This is not she.

This was her house in which she lived.
This was her set of tools with which she worked.

I love this frail shell lying in the pink-lined casket,
I love it because she once lived there,
    because she once used those
    hands,
    eyes,
    mouth,
    feet
    to care for me and give me love.

But this is not she.
She is far away.
But all about us still savoring the new adventure,
    life eternal.
Laughing, caring, relishing, in a dimension
    we cannot conceive.

Weep tears of sorrow for our temporary loss,
    but do not weep tears of finality,
    for we will see her again.

Weep tears of pain at our separation,
    but do not weep tears for my mother.
This is her Coronation Day.

My uncle preached the sermon; my oldest brother read her letter to me about death as we gathered around the casket in the cemetery. Her body was laid to rest in the quiet little village of Morgan Mill. On the stone, we had inscribed:

Here lies as much Goodness
As can die.

A mother gives birth to her children; goes with them through all of life's changing seasons; teaches them lessons of war, peace, getting, losing, mourning, healing, rending, sewing; but perhaps her finest gift is when her children can stand at her grave and say, "She was a good woman, but she is not dead. Here lies as much Goodness as can die."

This is a gift of faith, of strength that comes when children face A TIME TO DIE.

Epilogue

IS NOT MY VOICE MY OWN?

I stand here in my kitchen, stirring milk into the "chocolaty" recesses of my mixing bowl, and singing "My Faith Looks Up to Thee." The morning sunlight pours like dancing gossamer threads through my open window, tasting with delight the batter that will make a chocolate cake for the little boys who watch me in eager anticipation. But suddenly I pause! My song slips away. And I wonder: Is not my voice my own?

My mind skips back, and I remember someone else who stood in a kitchen in the early morning sunlight, stirring milk into the batter of a chocolate cake and singing "My Faith Looks Up to Thee." It seems for a moment that I have slipped away and another is housed within my body. I look about the kitchen. I know it is I, yet it is so familiar! It is so much a part of something I knew long ago.

It was my mother who used to sing this song while she combined the ingredients of a chocolate cake. And I was the child who sat watching and listening to her voice as it soared in melody.

Now I am in her footsteps. I have taken her place in the kitchen and I sing her song.

IS NOT MY LAUGHTER MY OWN?

I stand on the wide expanse of green; inhale the air, heavily scented with flowers; look into the lush of the sunset; wave to the silvery clouds curling like petals, weaving the sky into a glorious pattern of pink and white; watch my grass-stained children tasting the nectar in buttercups and caressing the lady-slippers' dainty toes; and I throw up my hands in rapture, laughing in heart-filled joy at the sheer beauty of it all.

I have seen someone else stand in the meadow, laughing with joyousness at the beauty of God's world. I have seen someone else grab up a child, still tinged with the yellow of buttercups and hold him to her heart in a sudden surge of loving delight.

But . . .

I was that child, and it was my mother who laughed.

And now I am in her footsteps. I have taken her place upon the great expanse of grassy beauty, and I laugh with joy.

ARE NOT MY HANDS MY OWN?

I go to church on Sunday and I sit at the dark-stained piano; my fingers slip over the ivory keys, calling the people to worship. While the congregation—and the little boys on the front seat—sing the grand old songs of praise to God, my hands form the chords, the arpeggios, and the melody of the hymns. The music—which fills the church, swells to its rafters, and rises into the blueness of the cobalt sky—comes from the movement of my hands.

But wait! Suddenly it seems that my hands are used only as a glove. I sense that another has slipped into my frame and is using my hands, my fingers, my muscles—making them move according to her will. And from them come glorious chords of harmony that ascend heavenward, carrying in their beauty the hearts and souls of worshiping people.

I look at my hands. They are my own. But I have seen another's hands play these same songs in church. With a deep, full knowledge, I know her inner feelings of worship and adoration as she played upon the keys. It was my mother who played the piano for church; I, her child, sat on the front seat and listened.

Now I am in her footsteps. I have taken her place upon the piano bench, and my hands play for church.

IS NOT MY TEACHING MY OWN?

I sit upon the bed with my pajama-clad children and read to them a story about a boy who gave his all to Jesus. Jesus took the boy's small gift and made it big enough to bless thousands. And I try to teach my children about the beauty of Jesus Christ.

But I can remember a little girl in a pink gown sitting on the foot of the bed, listening to her mother read this same story. I can catch the same inflections in the voice, the same detail in enunciation, the same light of love surrounding the name of Jesus. That was my mother and I was the little girl.

I have taken her place upon the bed, telling wide-eyed, impressionable children about the Man of Galilee.

AM I NOT MY OWN?

There is much in me that was my mother; I, who idolized her, followed along in her steps. At first her steps were too large for me, and the gap between each step was too wide for me to seem to be following at all. But after a short time—such a short time—my feet fitted the mold, and my stride matched hers.

Then for awhile I thought that I trod a new path, until one day I realized I was only walking in her footsteps, following in the path she had trod before.

In the evening breeze I stand in the dimly lighted bedroom and look upon the sleeping forms of my two little sons.

Softly I quote the lines of the poem:

> There followeth after me today
> A child whose feet must pass this way.

I go to my knees beside their beds, begging for guidance, wisdom, and grace that these who follow in my footsteps will be led, as I was, to the Almighty God.